LET'S PLAY

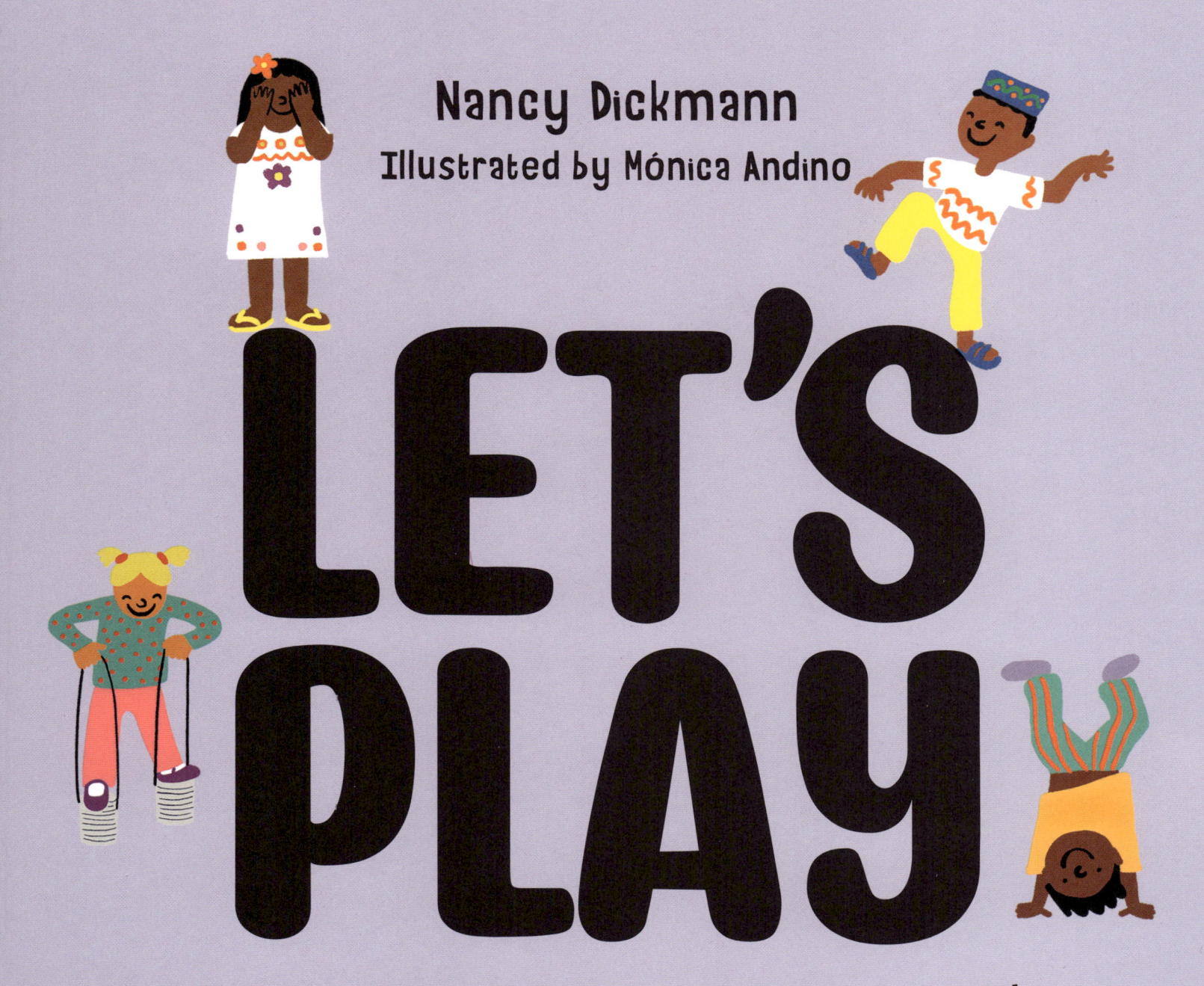

Nancy Dickmann
Illustrated by Mónica Andino

Children's games from around the world

words&pictures

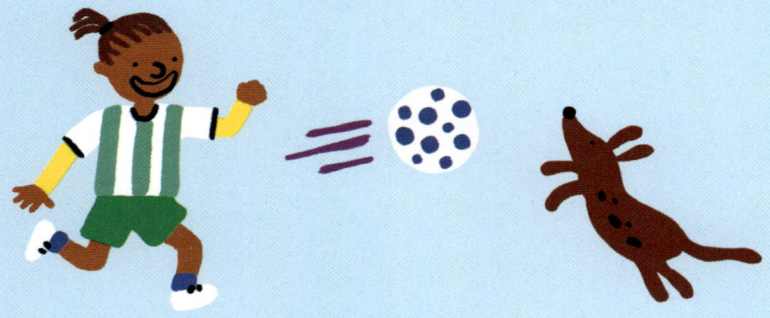

© 2023 Quarto Publishing Group USA Inc.
Text © Nancy Dickmann 2023
Illustrations © Monica Andino 2023

First published in 2023 by words & pictures,
an imprint of The Quarto Group.
100 Cummings Center,
Suite 265D Beverly, MA 01915, USA.
T (978) 282-9590 F (978) 283-2742
www.quarto.com

Assistant Editor: Alice Hobbs
Designer: Kathryn Davies
Art Director: Susi Martin
Associate Publisher: Holly Willsher

No part of this publication may be reproduced,
stored in a retrieval system, or transmitted in any form or by any
means, electronic, mechanical, photocopying, recording, or otherwise,
without the prior permission of the publisher, nor be otherwise
circulated in any form of binding or cover other than that in which
it is published and without a similar condition being imposed
on the subsequent purchaser.

All rights reserved.

A CIP record for this book is available from the Library of Congress.

ISBN: 978-0-7112-8376-3

Manufactured in Guangdong, China TT052023

9 8 7 6 5 4 3 2 1

CONTENTS

4

Time to Play!

10

Games for One Player

16

Games for Two Players

28

Games for Three to Five Players

42

Games for Big Groups

62

Make Your Own!

64

Index

TIME TO PLAY

Children around the world may wear different clothes, speak different languages, and eat different foods, but there is one thing they all have in common. They all play!

Playing is any activity done for fun, and it's an important part of growing up. Even animals like baby lions play. For them, it's a way of having fun as well as learning skills that they'll need when they start to hunt. And for humans, it's not so different! At the same time as you're having fun, you get to exercise and learn how to interact and get along with others.

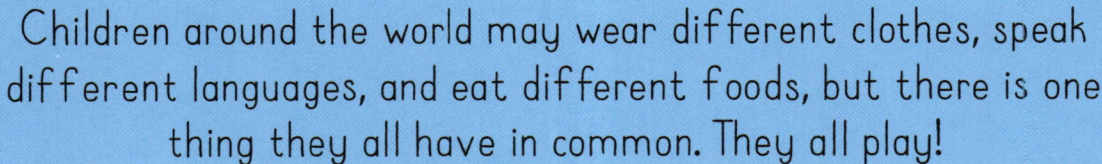

GAMES AROUND THE WORLD

Have you ever played tag? How about hide-and-seek or duck, duck, goose? These popular games are played in many different places. The names might change, or the rules might be slightly different. But the basic ideas stay the same, and most kids know how to play these games. So far, so good…but what about kubb, or luta de galo, or oonch neech? These games are popular in other parts of the world.

Each culture has its own traditional games. Some are quiet and based on clever strategies, while others are fast-paced and silly. Some are new, while others have been played for many years. This book will take you on a world tour to find enjoyable games to try for yourself. There is a world of fun just waiting to be discovered!

Are you ready to play?

HOW TO USE THIS BOOK

Each page in this book features a different game, so you can dip in and out to find something fun to do. The games are organized into chapters, depending on how many players you need—from simple games to play on your own or with one friend, to ones that work best with a lot of people. No matter what size your group, you can go straight to the chapter you need to find something fun to play.

WHERE TO PLAY

The fact file near the top of each page will give you important information. For example, some games are fine to play inside, while others work better outdoors. Games like hopscotch can be played in a fairly small area, while others that involve a lot of running will need a much bigger space. Before you start, check the fact file to see how much space you will need.

WHAT YOU NEED

You don't need any special equipment to play a game like tag, but this isn't the case for all games. Some need a ball, or a handkerchief, or tokens or counters. The fact file will tell you if any special equipment is needed for each game. Most of the items you need will be simple and easy to find around the house.

WHERE IN THE WORLD?

Each fact file will show you what country the game comes from. Can you find it on a map? Some games are played in several different places around the world, and this is usually explained in the text. You'll also find interesting facts about the games and how they link to each culture.

GREECE

GETTING STARTED

A lot of games start with one player being "it" or having some sort of special role. In other games, players take turns. Sometimes it's hard to agree on who gets to be "it," or who should go first. It's easy to settle this by playing a quick round of rock-paper-scissors. This game chooses a winner between two players, a bit like tossing a coin. It began in China many centuries ago, but it has spread around the world.

HOW TO PLAY

Two players face each other. On the count of three, each one holds out a hand making a specific shape.

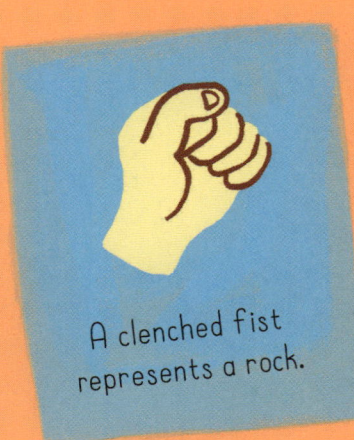

A clenched fist represents a rock.

A flat hand shows paper.

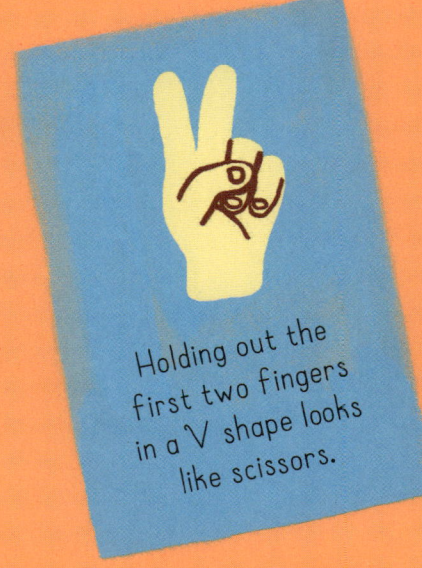

Holding out the first two fingers in a V shape looks like scissors.

The game is fair because each shape has an equal chance of winning. All three shapes will beat one of the others, but lose to the third.

8

Rock beats scissors because a heavy rock could smash a pair of scissors.

Paper beats rock because a piece of paper can cover a rock.

Scissors beats paper because a pair of scissors can cut through paper.

If both players show the same hand shape, it's a draw and they try again. If you have a big group, keep playing one-on-one rounds until only one winner is left.

WHAT'S IN A NAME?

In English this game is sometimes called Rochambeau or roshambo, though no one is quite sure why. In many languages the name is a direct translation of "rock-paper-scissors"—such as steen-papier-schaar in Dutch. But in others, it's completely different! In Japanese it's called janken or jankenpon. In French it's chi-fou-mi because this sounds like the Japanese for "one-two-three."

GAMES FOR ONE PLAYER

It's raining, and you're stuck inside with no one to play with and nothing to do. Or maybe you just need some quiet time, or a bit of a break from other people.

Whatever the reason, sometimes you need a game that will keep you entertained on your own. Luckily, there are plenty of options for one person! We often think of games as something that people do together, but you don't always need a group. Card games like solitaire are a good example. So are jigsaw puzzles and online games like Minecraft.

Here are some one-player games from around the world.

JEGICHAGI

This game is played with a toy called a "jegi," traditionally made from a piece of paper and a coin with a hole in the center. You can make your own!

 SOUTH KOREA | INDOORS OR OUTDOORS | CRAFT SUPPLIES | ACTIVE PLAY | 1+ PLAYERS

1 Using paper or plastic cut from a grocery bag, cut two squares measuring about 12 in on each side. Lay one on top of the other.

2 Put a few coins in the center and gather up the sides. Tie them with a piece of string, just above the coins.

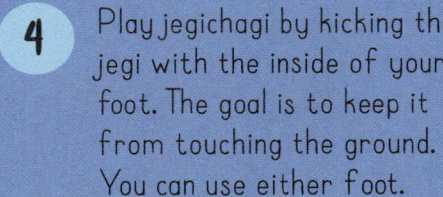

This game used to be played around the time of the New Year celebrations in South Korea. Now it is played all year round!

3 Cut the rest of the paper or plastic into strips and fan them out. Your jegi is finished!

4 Play jegichagi by kicking the jegi with the inside of your foot. The goal is to keep it from touching the ground. You can use either foot.

You can also play jegichagi with friends. Try passing the jegi around a circle, or see who can get the most kicks without dropping it.

11

TCHUKA RUMA

This game looks simple, but it's hard to get right! The goal is to get all eight of your counters into the "ruma" section at the end of the board.

 INDONESIA | INDOORS | PEN, PAPER, COUNTERS | BOARD GAME | 1 PLAYER

1 Cut a strip of paper or card stock and mark lines to divide it into five equal squares. Write "Ruma" in the last square.

2 Put two counters (such as coins or buttons) into each of the four empty squares.

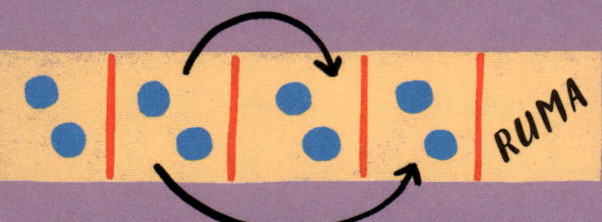

3 Choose a square and pick up both counters. Place them in the next squares, one in each.

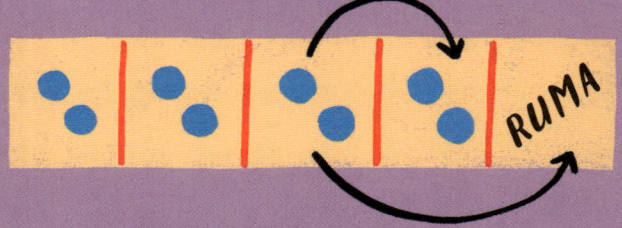

4 If the last counter lands in the ruma, go again by repeating step 3.

> If you've ever played a game called mancala, this might sound familiar. Similar games are played in many countries, usually by two players.

5 If the last counter lands in a square that already has counters, pick up all the counters for your next turn.

6 If the last counter lands in an empty square, you lose!

TANGRAMS

This puzzle is all about arranging smaller shapes to form a larger one. The possibilities are endless, so you can let your imagination run wild!

CHINA | INDOORS | CARD STOCK, PEN, RULER, SCISSORS | PUZZLE GAME | 1 PLAYER

1 Use a ruler to copy this template onto a square piece of card stock. (Tip: measure the half way point on each side to use as a guide.)

2 Cut out your shapes and mix them up. Can you remember how to put them back together to form a square?

3 Look at these animal shapes. Can you figure out how to arrange your seven pieces to form each animal? You can find lots more tangram puzzles online.

4 Try using your pieces to invent your own shapes. You can make objects, or even numbers or letters! The challenge is to use all seven pieces in each shape.

According to legend, tangrams are based on the work of the Chinese mathematician Liu Hui. He lived in the 3rd century CE and used geometric shapes to explain math concepts.

TRIPAS DE GATO

The name of this Mexican game means "cat guts," but don't worry—no animals are harmed! The name comes from the twisting lines you draw—they look a bit like your insides!

MEXICO | INDOORS | PEN AND PAPER | PUZZLE GAME | 1+ PLAYERS

This game can also be played with a friend. Take turns connecting the pairs. The first person who can't make a connection is the loser.

1. On a piece of paper, write the numbers 1 to 10, spread out randomly across the page.

2. Do it again so that there are two of each number.

3. Start with the ones, and draw a line to connect them.

4. Now try to do the same with the remaining pairs of numbers. But beware! Your line is not allowed to cross or touch any of the other lines.

5. How many pairs can you connect before you get stuck?

You don't have to use numbers in this game. You can use words, shapes, or emojis! Anything will work as long as they come in pairs.

POSICIÓN EN LATAS

Have you ever wanted to be taller? Here's your chance! Children in many countries make stilts from old cans. In Brazil, the word "latas" means "cans."

 BRAZIL | INDOORS OR OUTDOORS | CANS, STRING | ACTIVE PLAY | 1 PLAYER

1. Find and rinse out two large cans that are the same size.

2. Ask an adult to make two holes opposite each other, just below the lid.

3. Run a piece of string or rope (at least 30 in long) through the holes and tie it to make a loop.

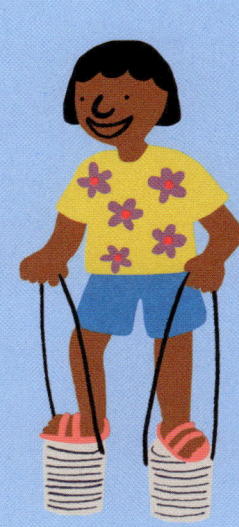

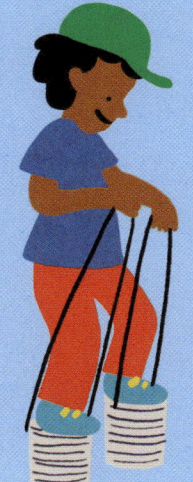

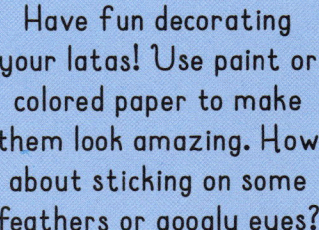

Have fun decorating your latas! Use paint or colored paper to make them look amazing. How about sticking on some feathers or googly eyes?

4. When your two "stilts" are ready, try walking on them. Put one foot on each can and hold the string loops in your hands.

5. Lift with your hand at the same time as you lift your foot. How far can you go?

15

GAMES FOR TWO PLAYERS

One is fun, but two is twice as nice!

If you have a friend or a sibling to play with, there are a lot more games open to you. In some of these games, you and your partner are competing against each other. In others, you work together.

How competitive are you feeling today?

Here are some two-player games from around the world to try. Most of these games don't take very long to play, so if you lose, don't worry—just ask for a rematch. And if you win, don't rub it in too much! Remember that winning is nice, but the main goal is to have fun with your friend.

CHOOSE THE STONE

In this simple game, one player chooses a number and the other player has to guess what it is. All they have to help them is two rows of stones, so they have to think carefully!

| LIBERIA | INDOORS OR OUTDOORS | STONES OR COUNTERS | PUZZLE GAME | 2 PLAYERS |

1 Find 16 stones or counters and write a number on each, from 1 to 16. Arrange them in numerical order, in 2 rows of 8.

2 One player chooses a number but doesn't tell the other.

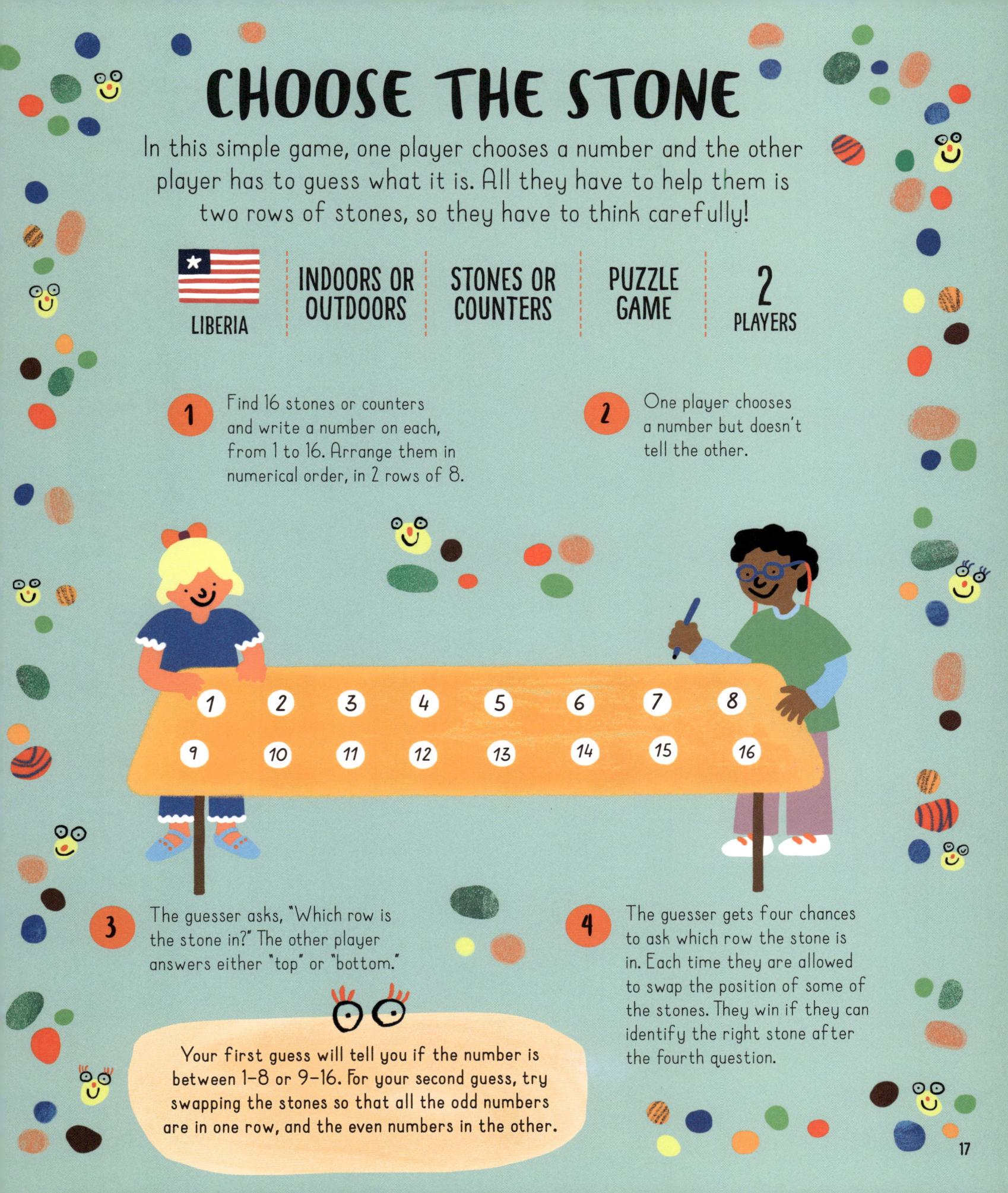

3 The guesser asks, "Which row is the stone in?" The other player answers either "top" or "bottom."

4 The guesser gets four chances to ask which row the stone is in. Each time they are allowed to swap the position of some of the stones. They win if they can identify the right stone after the fourth question.

Your first guess will tell you if the number is between 1–8 or 9–16. For your second guess, try swapping the stones so that all the odd numbers are in one row, and the even numbers in the other.

DOWN, DOWN, DOWN

How good are you at playing catch? Your skills will be tested to the limit in this fun Australian game!

AUSTRALIA | **OUTDOORS** | **TENNIS BALL** | **THROWING GAME** | **2 PLAYERS**

1 Stand about 10 steps away from your partner, facing each other. Start throwing the ball back and forth.

2 When someone drops the ball, say: "Down!" They have to go down on one knee.

3 The second time someone drops the ball, they go down on both knees. The third time, an elbow goes down, then the second elbow the next time.

4 Finally, it's down on their chin. If they miss the ball again, they're out!

You can make this game harder by using a larger ball, or by taking a step backward each time someone catches it. Or on a hot day, you could try it with a water balloon. Just be prepared to get wet!

THE EXQUISITE CORPSE

You never know quite what you'll get with this game! It was invented by artists about 100 years ago as a way to be creative, random...and a bit silly.

FRANCE | INDOORS | PENCIL AND PAPER | CREATIVE PLAY | 2+ PLAYERS

1 Secretly write a few words or a sentence at the top of a piece of paper.

2 Fold the paper down so that your writing is hidden, then pass it to your partner.

3 They will write more secret words and fold them down before passing it back to you.

4 Continue writing back and forth until you're ready to read out the finished work. It may not make much sense!

5 You can also do this with pictures. Try drawing a body where you draw the head, your partner draws the torso, you draw the legs, and they draw the feet.

This game's bizarre name has a simple explanation. One of the first times the artists played it, the sentence they produced was "The exquisite corpse will drink the new wine." They liked it so much that the name stuck!

19

MAKE THE STICK JUMP

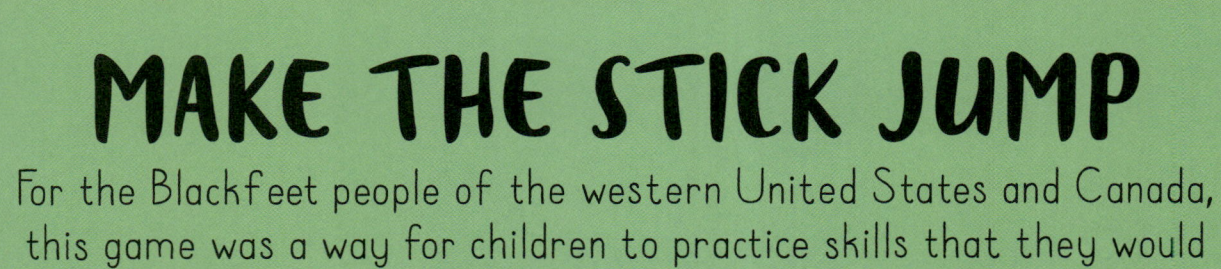

For the Blackfeet people of the western United States and Canada, this game was a way for children to practice skills that they would need for learning to hunt.

BLACKFEET NATION | **LARGE GRASSY AREA** | **CRAFT SUPPLIES** | **THROWING GAME** | **2+ PLAYERS**

Traditionally, Blackfeet children would cut willow sticks to play this game. Whenever they cut one, the plant had to be honored or thanked, often by leaving a gift in the ground.

1 Find five sticks of a similar size. Decorate them by tying on beads or feathers.

2 Ask an adult to cut notches or rings into the sticks. One stick should have one mark, one should have two, and so on. The marks show how many points the sticks are worth.

3 Poke the sticks into the ground so they are standing up. They should be arranged in a line, with the one-point stick closest to the throwing area and the five-point stick farthest away.

4 Take it in turns throwing a ball, beanbag, or hacky sack, and try to knock the sticks over. Add up your points to see who won!

With your partner, agree how many throws you get for each turn and how many points you need to win. In some versions, you have to knock the first stick down before you can aim for the second.

CONKERS

Finding conkers on the ground is a fall tradition. These glossy brown seeds come from the horse chestnut tree and are sometimes called "buckeyes" or "chesnuts." Children have played this game for years.

 UNITED KINGDOM | INDOORS OR OUTDOORS | CRAFT SUPPLIES | PLAY FIGHTING | 2 PLAYERS

1 Find a few conkers to use. Look for ones that are round and hard.

2 Ask an adult to help you make a hole through the center. Thread a piece of string or a shoelace through the hole and tie a knot to keep the conker from falling off.

3 One player dangles their conker from the string, holding it as still as they can.

4 The other player swings their conker and tries to hit the other one. After three misses, the other player gets to try.

5 You win by breaking the other player's conker.

Test your conkers by putting them in water. If a conker floats, it's more likely to crack. Choose one that sinks. The harder your conker, the better. Some people soak them in vinegar or bake them in the oven.

21

LUTA DE GALO

In Portuguese, "luta de galo" means "rooster fight," and that's what this game is supposed to imitate...except that roosters don't usually hop on one leg!

  OUTDOORS HANDKERCHIEFS PLAY FIGHTING 2 PLAYERS

BRAZIL

1. Each player tucks a handkerchief or scarf into their waistband or front pocket. There should be enough left hanging out to grab.

2. Both players cross an arm across their chest—their right arm if they're right-handed, their left if they're left-handed. This arm can't be used.

3. Hop on one leg and try to grab your opponent's scarf.

In Brazil, people used to watch roosters fight for entertainment. But this is not kind to the animals, and it was banned nearly 100 years ago.

4. You win by grabbing the other player's scarf. Anyone who puts their foot down or uncrosses their arm loses automatically.

SERSO

Sometimes the best games are the simplest ones. Serso is basically a game of catch, but using hoops and sticks instead of a ball.

POLAND | OUTDOORS | HOOPS AND STICKS | THROWING GAME | 2 PLAYERS

1
You'll need two sticks, about 12 in long, and a circular hoop. You could make the hoop out of wire, or bend flexible branches like willow.

2
Stand facing your partner, about 10 steps apart. Each person holds a stick.

3
Using your free hand, throw the hoop to your partner. They try to catch it on their stick.

4
They throw the hoop back for you to catch on your stick.

KUBB

This game is sometimes called "Viking Chess." Perhaps that's because the Vikings had a fierce reputation, and kubb involves throwing sticks at each other!

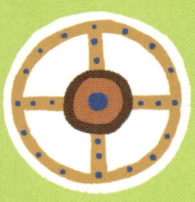

| SWEDEN | LARGE GRASSY AREA | A KUBB SET | THROWING GAME | 2+ PLAYERS |

1 Use the corner stakes to mark out the court, then stand 5 wooden blocks along each end. The king goes in the middle.

2 One player throws batons from their baseline, trying to knock down their opponent's blocks. You get 6 batons per turn.

3 When it's the second player's turn, they have to throw any of their blocks that got knocked down onto the court past the king, then stand them up and knock them down first before aiming at the first player's back row.

4 If a player fails to knock down all of the blocks in the middle of the court, their opponent gets to stand by the closest one for their next turn.

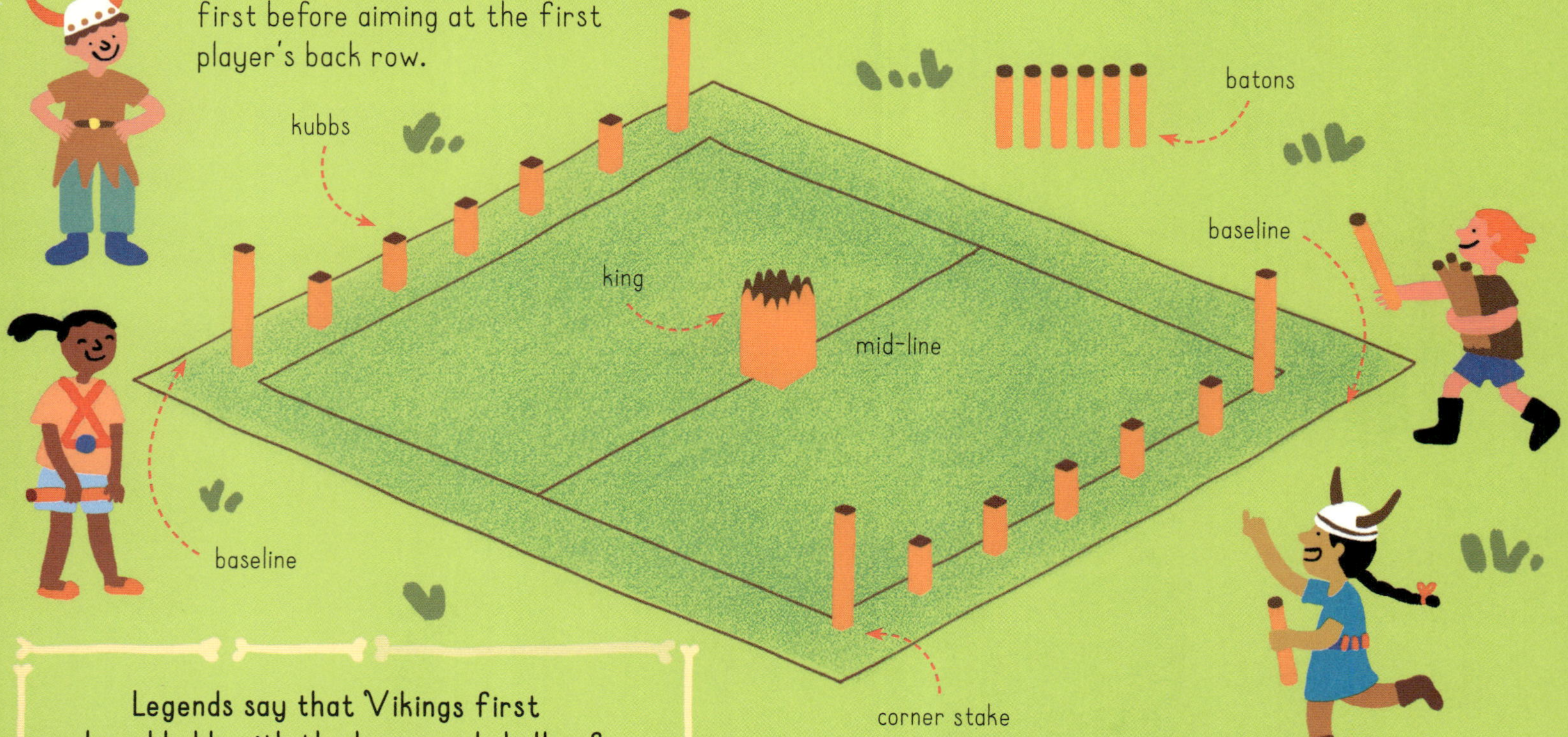

kubbs
king
mid-line
batons
baseline
baseline
corner stake

Legends say that Vikings first played kubb with the bones and skulls of their enemies! This is just made up, and although the game dates back at least 100 years, it is not as old as the Vikings.

5 Once you knock down all of your opponent's blocks, you aim for the king. Knock it down and you win!

KOLOWIS AWITHLAKNANNAI

This game is sometimes called "fighting serpents." It's a bit like checkers, because the goal is to capture all of your opponent's pieces by jumping over them.

ZUNI PUEBLO | INDOORS | PEN, PAPER, COUNTERS | BOARD GAME | 2 PLAYERS

1 Draw a game board with 16 pairs of triangles.

2 Each player has 23 counters. They put 16 on the points of the row closest to them, and 7 on the middle row, starting in one from the end. Only the middle and end points of the middle row are left empty.

3 The first player moves a counter one space into the empty space in the middle row.

4 The second player can jump that counter and remove it from the board.

5 Keep taking turns jumping your opponent's counters and taking them. Each move must be a jump, but multiple jumps are allowed.

6 If you capture all of your opponent's pieces, you win! If you both run out of moves, the player with more pieces left on the board wins.

The Zuni lived in the southwestern United States, in apartment blocks called pueblos. They used their roofs as terraces. This would have made a perfect place to play this game!

25

DDAKJI

Have you ever tried origami? You can make your own tiles for this game by folding paper squares. Then it's time to challenge your opponent!

SOUTH KOREA | INDOORS OR OUTDOORS | COLORED PAPER | THROWING GAME | 2 PLAYERS

1 Fold paper to make your ddakji tiles. You need two squares of different color paper (about 3 sq in) for each tile, and you'll need to make several tiles.

2 Play rock-paper-scissors to choose who gets to throw first. The other player puts their tile on the floor.

3 The first player tries to flip the tile over by throwing their own tile at it. If they succeed, they get to keep their opponent's tile. If they fail, they swap roles.

A  Fold each sheet into thirds.

B 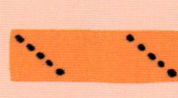 **C**  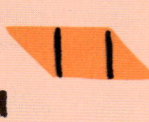 Fold one end up and the other down.

> It takes practice to find a good throwing technique. You have to throw your tile pretty hard! Stand up and try aiming for the center of the tile on the floor.

D  Lay one piece over the other.

E 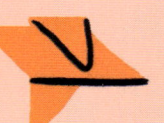 Fold the top down.

F  Fold the right side in.

G  Fold the bottom up.

H  Fold the left in and tuck it under.

SHIRITORI

This game is perfect for long car journeys. You can play it sitting still— and you only need your brain and someone to play with!

| JAPAN | INDOORS OR OUTDOORS | NO EQUIPMENT | WORD GAME | 2+ PLAYERS |

1 One player thinks of a word and says it out loud.

cat

2 The second player must come up with a word that starts with the last letter of the first word.

train

3 Now the first player has to use the last letter of their opponent's word.

nose

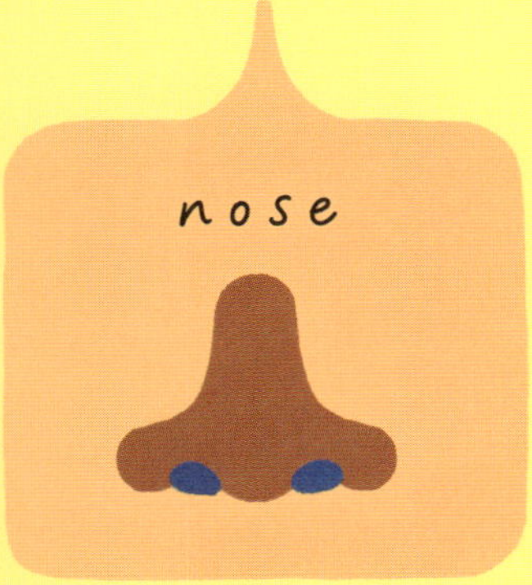

4 Keep taking turns, without repeating any words, until someone can't think of a word.

5 If this is too easy, add your own rules! You could set a time limit, or decide that each word must have a certain number of syllables, or limit it to a particular category, such as animals or food.

This game comes from Japan, where they don't use an alphabet like we do. Instead, they have 46 symbols that each represent a whole sound or syllable. This makes the game harder, because you have to match a syllable rather than just a single letter. Try playing it this way in English!

The word "cat"

27

GAMES FOR THREE TO FIVE PLAYERS

If you like playing board games, you've probably noticed that many of them are designed for small groups. A lot of other games—especially more active games—are too! Having a few players means you can play games with more different roles. And with four or more, you can even split up into teams.

For most of the games in this chapter, the number of players that can take part is flexible. As long as you have at least the minimum number, the game will work. And if you have more people who want to play… well then, the more the merrier!

NASCONDINO

If you've ever played hide-and-seek, then this game will feel familiar. It's a unique Italian twist on a classic children's favorite.

 ITALY | INDOORS OR OUTDOORS | NO EQUIPMENT | ACTIVE PLAY | 3+ PLAYERS

1 Choose one player to be "it" and choose a place to be the home base, called "tana" in Italian.

2 The person who is "it" closes their eyes and counts slowly to 30. Everyone else finds a hiding place.

3 When "it" finishes counting, they look for the others. When they find someone, they run back to the home base and announce the name of the person they found. The first one they find will be "it" in the next round.

4 The other players can stay hidden, or they can make a break for the home base. If they make it without being tagged, they shout "libero!"

5 If the last person makes it safely back to base and shouts "liberi tutti!" (meaning "everyone's free!"), then all the caught players are set free, and the same person has to be "it" again in the next round.

Did you know that Italy is home to the World Championships of hide-and-seek? People come from all over the world to compete.

TINIKLING

This activity from the Philippines is more of a dance than a game. There is no winner or loser, just a lot of fun!

PHILIPPINES | **INDOORS OR OUTDOORS** | **LONG WOODEN POLES** | **ACTIVE PLAY** | **3+ PLAYERS**

1. Find two poles of the same length—long bamboo canes are traditional, but broom handles will also work.

2. Two people crouch down, each holding one end of a pole in each hand.

3. Working together, they hit the poles on the ground, about shoulder-width apart. They do two hits like this, then slide the poles together for a third.

4. Continue the one-two-three rhythm—two beats with the poles apart followed by one with them together.

Find some music that you like and tap the poles in time to the beat. If you have 6 or more people, you can use two sets of poles, laid out like a cross.

5. The rest of the group take turns hopping and jumping through the poles when they are apart.

Search for videos of tinikling for inspiration. Some of the dances are very complicated! Can you make up your own routines?

CEVİZ OYUNU

This throwing game will test your hand-eye coordination as you try to win your friends' walnuts. If you're feeling brave you could even play with candies, but watch out—you might lose them if your aim is off!

| TURKEY | OUTDOORS | NAIL, COIN, WALNUTS | THROWING GAME | 3+ PLAYERS |

Ceviz is the Turkish word for "walnut." Turkey is one of the world's main producers of walnuts, and they are used in baklava and many other delicious treats!

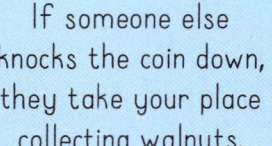
Baklava

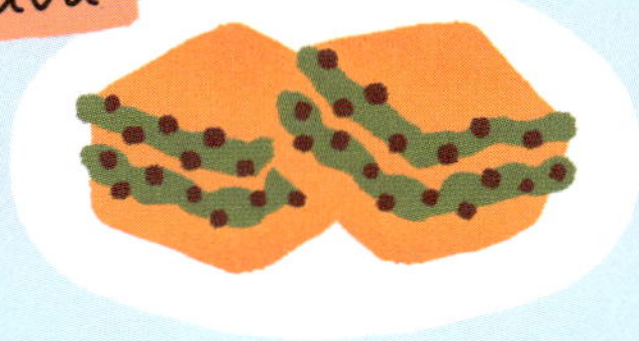

1 Get some walnuts and share them out equally, so that everyone has a handful. If you don't have walnuts, or if anyone you are playing with is allergic to nuts, you could use other things such as conkers, pebbles, or marbles.

2 Pound a nail into the ground and balance a coin on top.

3 Take it in turns throwing a walnut at the coin. If you knock it off, put it back in place and wait nearby. If anyone else misses the coin, you get to keep their walnut.

4 If someone else knocks the coin down, they take your place collecting walnuts.

5 The game ends when one player has all the walnuts.

HAJLA

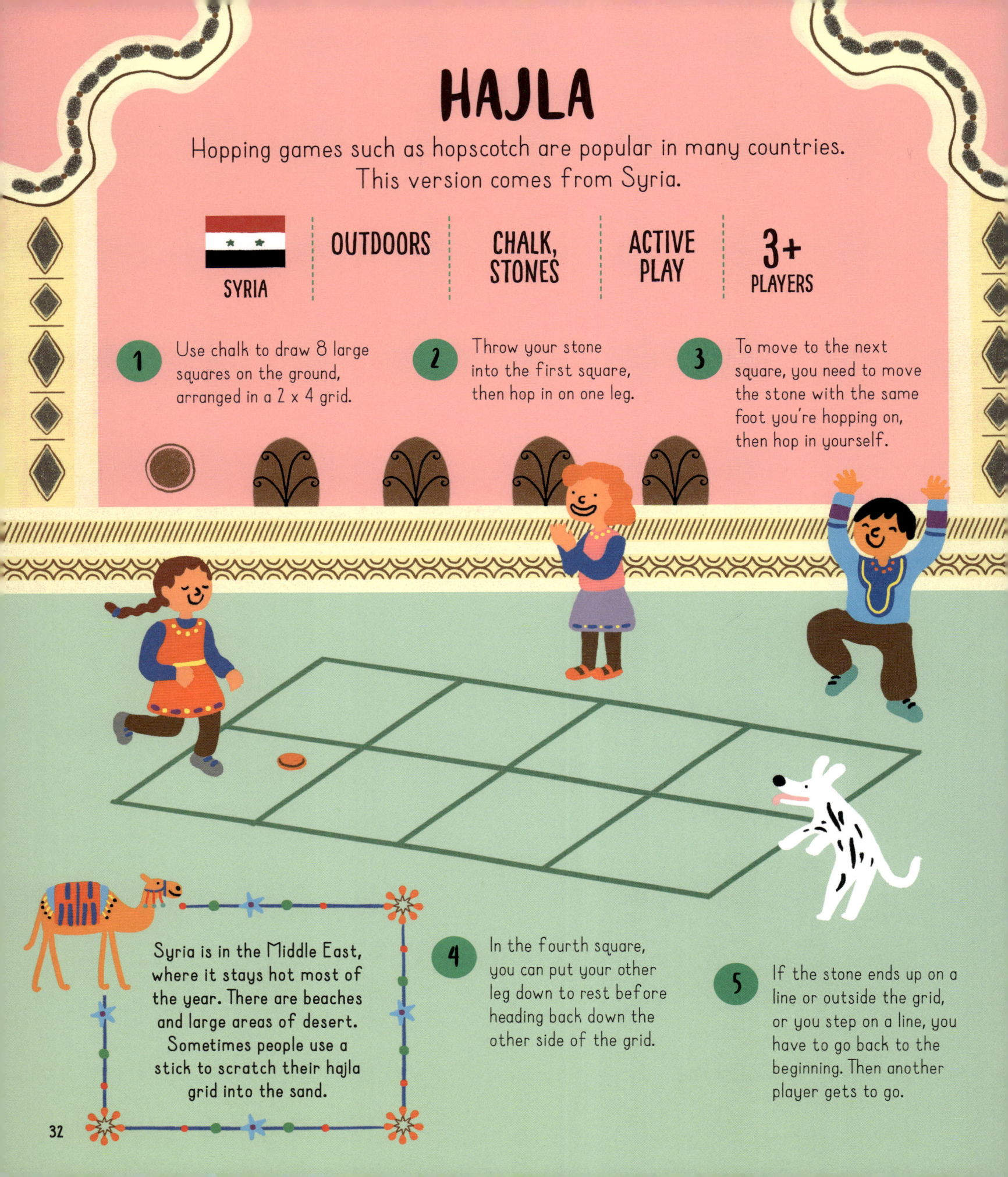

Hopping games such as hopscotch are popular in many countries. This version comes from Syria.

SYRIA | **OUTDOORS** | **CHALK, STONES** | **ACTIVE PLAY** | **3+ PLAYERS**

1. Use chalk to draw 8 large squares on the ground, arranged in a 2 x 4 grid.

2. Throw your stone into the first square, then hop in on one leg.

3. To move to the next square, you need to move the stone with the same foot you're hopping on, then hop in yourself.

4. In the fourth square, you can put your other leg down to rest before heading back down the other side of the grid.

5. If the stone ends up on a line or outside the grid, or you step on a line, you have to go back to the beginning. Then another player gets to go.

Syria is in the Middle East, where it stays hot most of the year. There are beaches and large areas of desert. Sometimes people use a stick to scratch their hajla grid into the sand.

32

DITHWAI

Farming is important in Lesotho, and a family's cattle are a sign of their wealth. But real cows are too big for this game, so children use stones instead!

LESOTHO | INDOORS OR OUTDOORS | STONES, STICKS/CRAFT STICKS | MEMORY GAME | 3+ PLAYERS

This is a good example of a game that helps children practice skills they will need as adults. They learn to be observant, which will help them recognize their family's cattle.

1 Each player finds 10 small stones and uses sticks or soil to make a pen (called a "kraal") to hold them. (Use building bricks or craft sticks if you're playing indoors.)

2 The first player says, "Let me examine my cattle." They look carefully at their stones, then they close their eyes. The other players each take one of the first player's stones and put it in their own kraal.

3 The first player opens their eyes and tries to recognize the stones that were taken. If they do, they can take them back. If they can't identify any of them, the other players get to keep them.

Let me examine my cattle.

4 The next player continues the game, and the winner is the player with the most stones at the end.

TAG

When it comes to games, you probably won't find one simpler than tag, where one player tries to catch another. Many versions have sprung up around the world. Each one is different, but they're all fun! Here are just a few.

 WORLDWIDE | OUTDOORS | NO EQUIPMENT | ACTIVE PLAY | 3+ PLAYERS

THE BASIC RULES

1. Choose one player to be "it."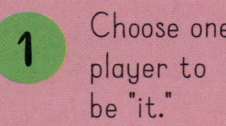
2. Everyone else runs away while "it" tries to tag them by touching them with a hand.
3. The person who gets tagged is now "it," and the game continues.

ELBOW TAG

1. Start with one "it" and one runner. Everyone else finds a partner and links arms at the elbow.
2. The runner runs while "it" chases them. The runner will be safe if they link arms with one of the pairs. 
3. When the runner links up with one person in a pair, the other person in that pair must break off and become the new runner.
4. Any runner who gets tagged is now "it", and the game continues.

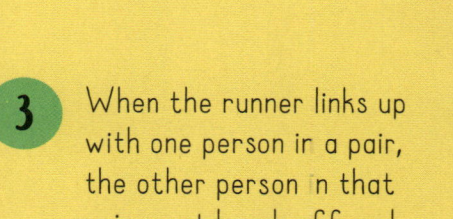

BALL TAG

1 Choose one player to be "it." They carry a soft ball.

2 Instead of touching the other players, "it" tags them by throwing the ball at them and hitting them.

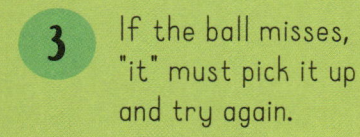

3 If the ball misses, "it" must pick it up and try again.

FREEZE TAG

1 Choose one player to be "it." They chase the other players.

2 When another player gets tagged, they don't become "it." Instead, they must freeze in place while "it" continues to chase the other players.

3 Any player can be "unfrozen" by being tagged by another player who is not "it."

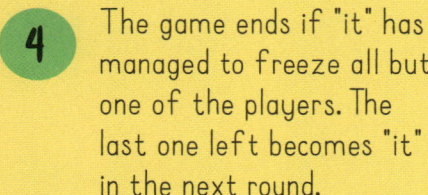

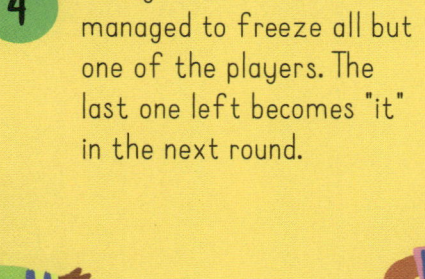

4 The game ends if "it" has managed to freeze all but one of the players. The last one left becomes "it" in the next round.

What kind of tag do you like to play? Can you invent your own version? What rules will you choose? You could have a home base where runners will be safe, or make a rule that when you are tagged you can't immediately tag back.

35

FEUER, WASSER, STURM, BLITZ

The name of this game is German for "fire, water, storm, lightning." But the nice thing is that you can play it indoors, no matter what the weather!

GERMANY | **INDOORS OR OUTDOORS** | **NO EQUIPMENT** | **ACTIVE PLAY** | **3+ PLAYERS**

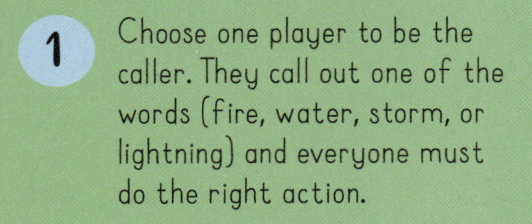

1 Choose one player to be the caller. They call out one of the words (fire, water, storm, or lightning) and everyone must do the right action.

2 If it's fire, you lie on the ground to escape the smoke and roll to put out the flames.

FIRE!

3 If it's water, you climb up onto something to escape the rushing water.

Can you add more words to the game? Think about other types of weather, such as rain or snow. What kind of actions would you do for them?

storm

lightning

water

4 If it's storm, you have to hold on to something solid so that you don't get blown away.

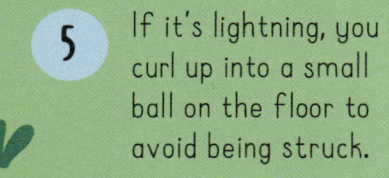

5 If it's lightning, you curl up into a small ball on the floor to avoid being struck.

6 The last player to do the right action is out. Continue until only one player is left.

36

JOGO DOS PÉS ATADOS

How do you make a race more fun? By making it harder, of course! In this "tied feet game," you have to work with a partner.

PORTUGAL | **LARGE SPACE** | **SCARVES** | **ACTIVE PLAY** | **4+ PLAYERS**

1 Set up a course with an obstacle at the far end, which players must go around.

2 Each player chooses a partner, so they are in pairs.

3 Each pair ties their legs together with a scarf, so that they are facing in the same direction and one player's right leg is tied to the other player's left.

4 When the race starts, the teams must race to the obstacle, go around it, and return to the starting point. The first team back is the winner.

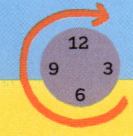

You can race with more than two pairs, but the course might get crowded. Why not split the pairs into two teams and do it as a relay race? Or each pair could run on their own, and you time them to see who gets the fastest time.

SARDINES

This fun (and very silly) game is a bit like hide-and-seek in reverse. The more players you have, the sillier it gets...but it will always make you laugh!

UNITED KINGDOM | **INDOORS OR OUTDOORS** | **NO EQUIPMENT** | **ACTIVE PLAY** | **4+ PLAYERS**

1. You need a big space with plenty of hiding places, such as a house or park. Make sure all the players know the boundaries.

2. Choose one player to hide.

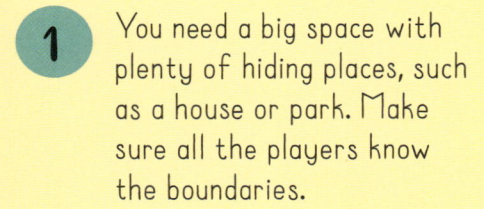

3. Everyone else closes their eyes and counts slowly to 30 while the player finds a hiding place.

4. Once you reach 30, everyone looks for the missing player. If you find them, quietly join them in their hiding place.

5. The game continues until everyone has found the hiding place and you are all squeezed in together! The last player to find it becomes the hider in the next round.

Have you ever opened up a tin of sardines? The little fish are packed in very tightly—just like you and your friends will be packed into your hiding place!

MUURBALL

This game comes from the Netherlands, where "muur" means "wall." It's a popular game for children to play on the school playground in small groups—or even large ones!

NETHERLANDS | **OUTDOORS** | **BOUNCY BALL** | **ACTIVE PLAY** | **4+ PLAYERS**

1 One player faces the wall, a few yards away, and stands with their feet slightly apart.

2 Everyone lines up behind them.

3 The player at the front throws a bouncy ball at the wall.

4 When it bounces back, they must jump over it, and everyone behind jumps over the ball too.

5 If the ball hits someone, they're out.

6 If no one gets hit, the thrower moves to the back and the player who was second in the line gets to throw.

Around the world, there are lots of different games that involve hitting a ball against a wall. They are popular because they don't need any equipment aside from a ball—after all, there are walls everywhere!

39

SALONOWIEC

The name of this game is pronounced sah-low-no-vee-ets, and it's Polish for "man about town." The game is similar to an American classroom game called "heads up seven up."

POLAND | **INDOORS OR OUTDOORS** | **NO EQUIPMENT** | **GUESSING GAME** | **3+ PLAYERS**

1 One player puts their head down on a table (or leans against a wall), closing their eyes. The other players line up behind them.

2 One player taps the person with their eyes closed on the shoulder.

3 Now the first player has to guess who tapped them on the shoulder. If they guess right, they swap places with the tapper. If they guess wrong, they keep getting tapped until they get it right.

The Lemko people from southeastern Poland play a version that is often called "backside beating." Instead of tapping the player on the shoulder, they_well, you can probably guess!

GHOST IN THE GRAVEYARD

In most versions of hide-and-seek, once you're found, you're out. But in this one, that's when the fun really begins!

UNITED STATES · **OUTDOORS** · **NO EQUIPMENT** · **ACTIVE PLAY** · **3+ PLAYERS**

ghost

1 You need a big outdoor space with lots of places to hide. Make sure everyone knows the boundaries.

2 Choose one area to be the home base, and choose one player to be the ghost.

3 Everyone stays at the home base with their eyes closed while the ghost hides. The players count slowly, "1 o'clock, 2 o'clock…" until they get to 12 o'clock. Then they shout, "Midnight, midnight! I hope I don't see a ghost tonight!"

Midnight, midnight! I hope I don't see a ghost tonight!

4 Everyone splits up to look for the ghost. The person who finds them shouts, "Ghost in the graveyard!"

5 The other players run back to base while the ghost tries to tag them. (The person who found the ghost is automatically safe.)

This game is a lot of fun played after dark with torches. It's spookier and ghostlier that way! Check with an adult first, though, to make sure you stay safe.

6 If the ghost catches someone, that player is the ghost in the next round. If they don't catch anyone, the last player back to base becomes the ghost.

GAMES FOR BIG GROUPS

Playing games is a great way to make friends. If you're playing a game that looks like fun, others might come up and ask to join in. So why not say yes? With some games, the more players you have, the more fun you have.

Many of the games in the previous chapter will also work with larger groups, even though they can be played with just a few people. The games in this chapter, though, are really designed for large groups. They often need big spaces and are ideal for parks or school playgrounds.

PILOLO

This game is all about searching, but you hunt for objects, not people. It's a bit like a competitive Easter egg hunt!

GHANA | **OUTDOORS OR INDOORS** | **STICKS** | **ACTIVE PLAY** | **5+ PLAYERS**

Ghanaian children often sing a traditional song as they hunt for the sticks. Its name means "nobody is expected to cry."

1 Choose one player to be the leader, and decide where the finish line will be.

2 The leader hides small sticks (at least one per person) while the other players close their eyes.

pilolo! — leader

3 When the leader shouts "pilolo!" the other players begin to look for the sticks.

4 When you find a stick, pick it up and head for the finish line. You can make a dash for it, or go more slowly so that the other players don't notice that you've found a stick.

5 Once everyone has found a stick, the leader gives out points. The first player to reach the finish line gets the most points.

6 After a few rounds, add up each player's points to find the winner!

You don't have to use sticks for this game. You can use stones, coins, marbles—anything really, as long as everyone knows what to look for.

43

OONCH NEECH

In the Urdu language spoken in Pakistan, "oonch" means "high" and "neech" means "low." That means that this fast-paced tag game is played on two levels!

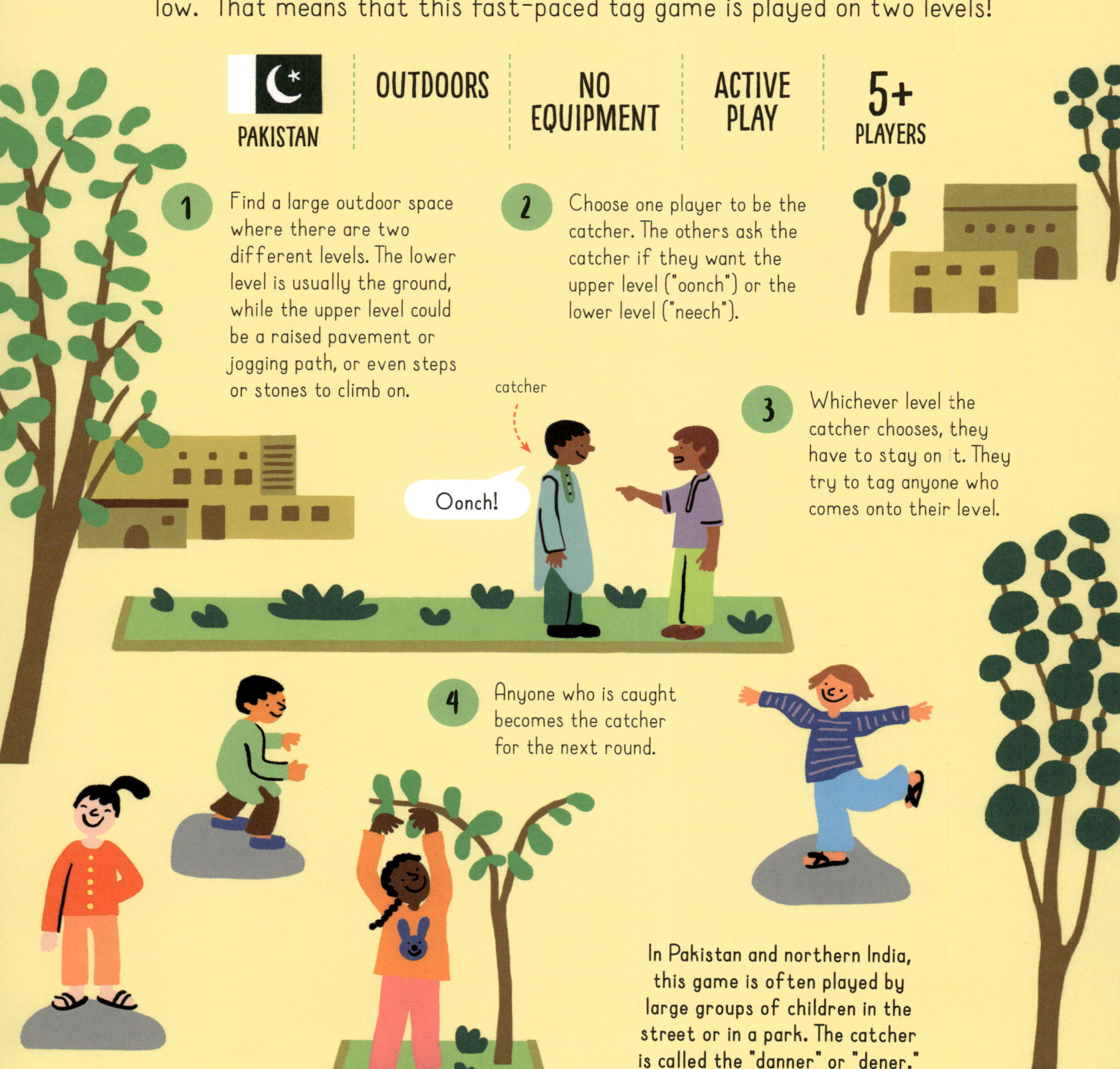

PAKISTAN | **OUTDOORS** | **NO EQUIPMENT** | **ACTIVE PLAY** | **5+ PLAYERS**

1. Find a large outdoor space where there are two different levels. The lower level is usually the ground, while the upper level could be a raised pavement or jogging path, or even steps or stones to climb on.

2. Choose one player to be the catcher. The others ask the catcher if they want the upper level ("oonch") or the lower level ("neech").

catcher

Oonch!

3. Whichever level the catcher chooses, they have to stay on it. They try to tag anyone who comes onto their level.

4. Anyone who is caught becomes the catcher for the next round.

In Pakistan and northern India, this game is often played by large groups of children in the street or in a park. The catcher is called the "danner" or "dener."

44

PASS THE PARCEL

People wrap presents so that they're a surprise—it's more fun when you're kept guessing! This game is popular at birthday parties. Everyone gets to share in the unwrapping, but only one player claims the prize.

UNITED KINGDOM | **INDOORS** | **PRIZES, PAPER, TAPE** | **PARTY GAME** | **4+ PLAYERS**

1 Prepare for this game by secretly wrapping a prize in many layers of paper. You can also put a small prize or candy in each of the extra layers of wrapping.

2 Ask a player or adult to play music (and be ready to stop it at a random point). All the remaining players sit in a circle, and they pass the parcel as music plays.

3 When the music stops, the player holding the parcel may unwrap one layer. If there is anything inside, they can keep it, and they remain in the game.

4 The parcel gets passed again as the music starts up.

5 Keep removing layers when the music stops until one player gets the prize.

Instead of putting candies in the extra layers, you could insert slips of paper with challenges on them. For example, each paper could have the name of an animal written on it, and the person who unwraps that layer has to imitate the animal while the other players guess.

STATUES

You may know this game by a different name—it has a lot of names! It's like a reverse version of tag, where only one player is the target and all the others try to tag them.

WORLDWIDE | **OUTDOORS** | **NO EQUIPMENT** | **ACTIVE PLAY** | **6+ PLAYERS**

THE BASIC RULES

red light!

1 Choose one player to be the caller. Everyone else is a statue, and they line up at the far end of the playing space. Their goal is to tag the caller.

2 When the caller turns their back, all the statues can move toward them. They can move as quickly or as slowly as they like.

3 If the caller turns around to face them, all the statues must freeze. If a statue is caught moving, they have to go back to the starting line.

4 The caller can move around if they like, while the statues are frozen.

5 The round ends when one of the statues gets close enough to tag the caller. That statue will be the caller in the next round.

CALLING OUT

In many versions of the game, the caller controls the statues by shouting out certain phrases, instead of just facing away and turning around. For example, in the United States they shout "green light!" to make the statues move and "red light!" to make them stop—just like traffic lights.

green light!

STATUES IN OTHER LANGUAGES

Here are some of the names used for this game in other countries:

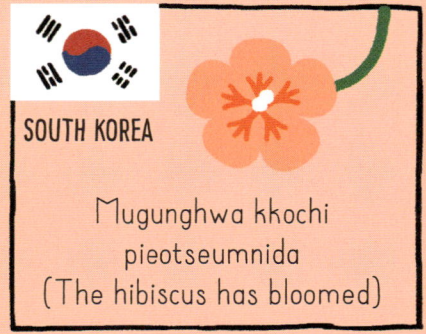

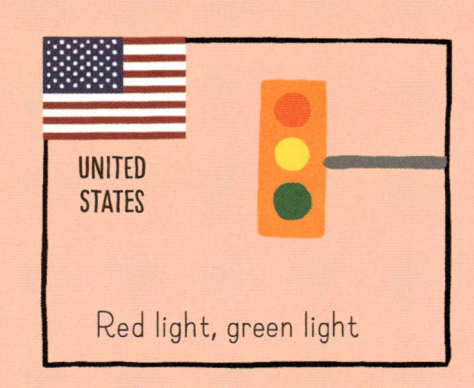

AUSTRIA
Donner, wetter, blitz!
(Thunder, weather, lightning)

CHILE
Un, dos, tres, momia es
(One, two, three, it's a mommy)

FRANCE
Un, deux, trois, soleil
(One, two, three, sun)

GERMANY
Eins, zwei, drei, ochs am berg (One, two, three, ox at the mountain)

ISRAEL
Dag maluah
(Pickled herring)

NETHERLANDS
Annemaria koekoek
(Peekaboo Annemaria!)

NEW ZEALAND
Sneak up granny

SINGAPORE
A, E, I, O, U

SOUTH KOREA
Mugunghwa kkochi pieotseumnida
(The hibiscus has bloomed)

UNITED KINGDOM
Grandmother's footsteps

UNITED STATES
Red light, green light

KABADDI

This fast-paced tagging game comes from India. It is popular with children, but adults play too—there is even a Kabaddi World Cup!

INDIA | **OUTDOORS** | **NO EQUIPMENT** | **ACTIVE PLAY** | **14+ PLAYERS**

1. Mark out a rectangular court on the ground, divided in half by a line.

2. Split into two equal teams. Each team takes one side of the court.

3. The teams take turns sending one player into the other half of the court as a "raider."

Raiders often shout "kabaddi" over and over while they run, to show that they are not breathing in. You can also use a stopwatch and limit raids to 30 seconds.

Raider

4. The raider tries to tag members of the other team, but they must do their entire raid in a single breath.

5. Any players that are tagged are out. The team gets one point for each person tagged.

6. The raider must return to their own side before their breath runs out, and the opposing team tries to stop them by grabbing or tackling. If they succeed, the raider is out.

7. Any time one team gets an opponent out, they can "revive" one of their own players who is sitting out.

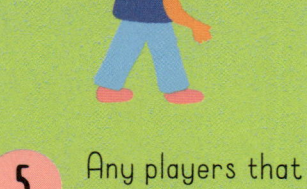

8. At the end of the game, the team with the most points wins.

SCHOKOLADENESSEN

This silly game, often played at birthday parties, is perfect for anyone who likes chocolate. If you're lucky, you'll get to eat a lot of it!

GERMANY | **INDOORS** | **CLOTHING, CHOCOLATE, CUTLERY, DICE** | **PARTY GAME** | **6+ PLAYERS**

You can make this game even harder by including a pair of bulky gloves with the dress-up clothes.

1 Prepare for the game by wrapping a bar of chocolate in several layers of paper.

2 Everyone sits around a table or in a circle on the floor, with the chocolate in the middle, along with a knife and fork. Put some dress-up accessories in the middle too, such as a hat, scarf, and sunglasses.

3 Players take turns rolling a dice. If someone rolls a six, they put on the silly clothes, then try to unwrap and eat the chocolate, using only the knife and fork.

4 While they work, the other players keep rolling the dice. If someone else rolls a six, they get to take over the clothes and the cutlery.

5 The game finishes when all the chocolate has been eaten!

Chocolate is very popular in Germany—the average person there eats about 17.6 pounds of chocolate per year!

49

BLIND MAN'S BUFF

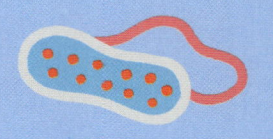

This game is basically a version of tag, where the job of the player who is "it" is made much harder by giving them a blindfold! It's a game that needs a big open space, free of obstacles that people might trip over. It is played all over the world.

WORLDWIDE | OUTDOORS | BLINDFOLD | ACTIVE PLAY | 6+ PLAYERS

THE BASIC RULES

1. Choose one player to be "it."

2. Put a blindfold on them, then spin them around a few times.

3. "It" has to find and tag another player, who then becomes "it" for the next round.

4. A slightly different version would be for the person who is "it" to have to find all the other players before handing over to someone else.

IMBUBE IMBUBE

In the Zulu language of southern Africa, "imbube" means "lion." In this version, the blindfolded player is the "lion" who tries to capture one other player (the "impala"). The rest of the players help the lion by chanting "imbube, imbube." They chant louder and faster if the lion is getting close to the impala. They chant slower and more quietly if the lion is getting farther away.

MARCO POLO

This version is popular in the United States, where it is often played in a swimming pool. The blindfolded person shouts "Marco!" and everyone else then replies "Polo!" The blindfolded player can use the sound of their voices to figure out where they are.

JOGO DA CABRA-CEGA

In Portugal, this game has a name meaning "blind goat game." The blindfolded player has to kneel down while the other players sing a song about cinnamon buns. When it is time for the blind goat to chase the other players, the goat must identify who they've caught by touch alone, and then that person will become the new blind goat.

FAIR PLAY

These games are a way of making tag harder for whoever is "it." That means it's not just about who can run the fastest! We all have different skills and abilities. How else could you change the rules of tag to make it fair for everyone?

CATCH THE DRAGON'S TAIL

This game is trickier than it seems at first! It involves holding on to each other and running around, so make sure everyone is comfortable and no one is being too rough. You will need a large outdoor space to play this game.

CHINA | **LARGE SPACE** | **NO EQUIPMENT** | **ACTIVE PLAY** | **8+ PLAYERS**

Unlike the typical image of a dragon in the West, Chinese dragons usually have long, snake like bodies.

1. Players line up behind one another and place their hands on the shoulders of the person in front.

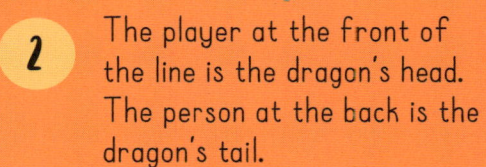

2. The player at the front of the line is the dragon's head. The person at the back is the dragon's tail.

3. The dragon's head must try to run around the back and catch the tail, while all the other players try to prevent them—without breaking the line!

4. If the dragon's head succeeds at catching the tail, they move to the back and become the tail. The person at the front is the new dragon's head. Keep playing until everyone has had a turn being the head and the tail.

Dragons are important in Chinese culture. They are associated with good luck and are thought to control the weather.

HALÁSZÁS

This is another high-energy game that involves teamwork.
Its name means "fishing" in Hungarian.

| HUNGARY | LARGE SPACE | NO EQUIPMENT | ACTIVE PLAY | 8+ PLAYERS |

1
Choose one person to be the fisher. All of the other players are fish—they run around trying to avoid the fisher, who must try to catch them.

2
When the fisher catches their first fish, the two players link arms and become the net. Then, the net must try to catch more fish.

3
Each player caught joins the net and helps to catch more fish. You can choose to play until only one fish is left, or until the net has caught everyone.

Fisher   Fish   Net

Hungary is a landlocked country in Central Europe. This means it has no coastlines, so fishing is done in lakes and rivers. Favorite fish to eat in Hungary are catfish and carp.

LA TOMATE

This popular playground game uses a ball to stand in for the tomato that it's named after. And it's a good thing too—it would be a lot messier and harder to play with a real tomato!

FRANCE | **OUTDOORS OR INDOORS** | **SOFT BALL** | **ACTIVE PLAY** | **5+ PLAYERS**

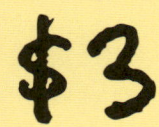

Tomate $3

Some children like to play a different version. If the ball goes between your legs, you must turn around and play the rest of the game facing out!

1 Players stand in a circle, facing inward. They spread their legs so that each foot touches their neighbor's foot, leaving no gaps in the circle.

2 They bend over, clasping their hands together and using them like a mallet to pass a ball back and forth across the circle.

3 The goal is to send the ball through another player's legs, while they use their clasped hands to try to block it.

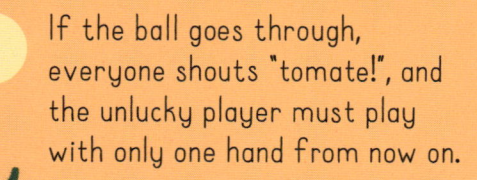

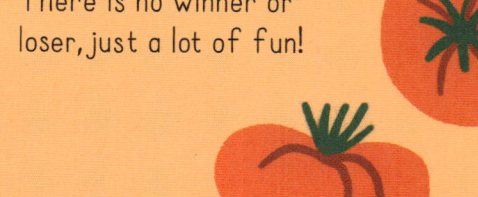

4 If the ball goes through, everyone shouts "tomate!", and the unlucky player must play with only one hand from now on.

5 There is no winner or loser, just a lot of fun!

JUGUEMOS EN EL BOSQUE

If you were being chased by a real wolf, it would be terrifying. But when it's just one of your friends pretending to be a wolf, it's loads of fun!

COLOMBIA | **OUTDOORS OR INDOORS** | **NO EQUIPMENT** | **ACTIVE PLAY** | **6+ PLAYERS**

1 Choose one player to be the wolf. The rest of the players form a circle around them, holding hands.

2 As they walk in a circle, the children say, "Let's play in the woods when the wolf is not there. Wolf, are you there?"

3 The wolf chooses an article of clothing and mimes putting it on while saying, "I'm putting on my…"

I'm putting on my coat!

4 The children keep asking the wolf the same question, and each time the wolf answers with a different item of clothing.

5 The game continues until the wolf decides to give a different answer: "Yes! I'm coming to eat you!"

6 The children scatter and the wolf tries to tag them. The first player the wolf catches will be the wolf in the next round.

In Colombia, children sing a traditional song in Spanish while they play this game. Can you find a video of it online? Try to learn it, or you can make up your own song instead.

CORRE, CORRE LA GUARACA

Take a look at the instructions for this game and see if it sounds familiar. It's very likely that you've played a version of it under a different name. This simple game is great for big groups and is played all over the world.

CHILE | **OUTDOORS OR INDOORS** | **HANDKERCHIEF** | **ACTIVE PLAY** | **6+ PLAYERS**

1 Choose one player to be "it." The rest of the players sit down in a circle.

2 The player who is "it" walks around the outside of the circle, holding a handkerchief, as everyone chants a rhyme.

3 Eventually the person who is "it" drops the handkerchief on someone's head or back, then takes off running around the circle.

4 The player with the handkerchief must grab it and chase after "it." If "it" reaches the place where the other player was sitting before being tagged, that player becomes the new "it."

DUCK, DUCK, GOOSE

In the United States, no handkerchief is used. Instead "it" taps each player on the head as they pass, saying "duck" for each one. When they reach the player that they want to choose, they say "goose" instead, then take off running. (In some regions, they give each "duck" a different color, and "gray duck" is the signal to start running.) This popular game was probably brought to the country by Swedish immigrants.

Duck!

THE POSTMAN

The version of the game played in France is called "Le facteur n'est pas passé," meaning "The postman hasn't passed." The person who is "it" plays the role of the postman, while the other players close their eyes and sing a song about the days of the week. During the song, the "postman" secretly delivers a parcel behind one of the children. When the song finishes, they all check to see who has it, and that person must chase the postman.

it

TELEPHONE

This is a good example of a game where a bigger group means more fun. The more people you have, the more garbled the message gets!

WORLDWIDE | **INDOORS OR OUTDOORS** | **NO EQUIPMENT** | **PARTY GAME** | **6+ PLAYERS**

This game is played in many different countries around the world, and it goes by a lot of different names: Operator, grapevine, pass the message, rumors, broken telephone, and stille post (quiet mail) are just a few of them.

1 All the players stand in a line.

2 The first player whispers a message to the person next to them, making sure that no one else can hear.

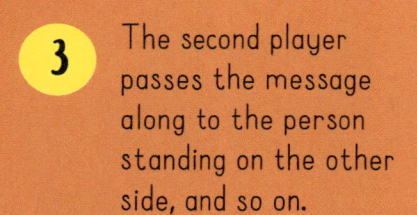

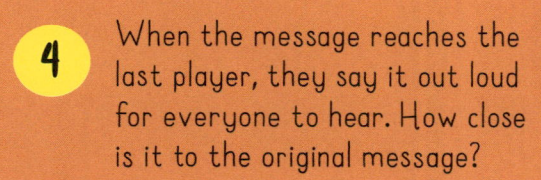

3 The second player passes the message along to the person standing on the other side, and so on.

4 When the message reaches the last player, they say it out loud for everyone to hear. How close is it to the original message?

5 There is no winner or loser, just a lot of laughter as you discover how much the message has changed as it's been passed on.

OPEN THE DOORS, YOUR MAJESTY

This is another game you may recognize. It's similar to "Oranges and lemons." Whichever version you play, you'll probably end up on the floor!

BULGARIA | **OUTDOORS** | **NO EQUIPMENT** | **ACTIVE PLAY** | **8+ PLAYERS**

1 Choose two players to be the leaders. They each choose a special code word—any word will do, such as "lemons" or "oranges."

2 The two leaders face each other and hold hands to form a gate that the rest of the players can pass through while singing a song.

3 When the song gets to the last line, the leaders bring their hands down to trap whichever player is underneath.

4 They quietly ask, "Do you want lemons or oranges?" Depending on whose code word the child chooses, they join that team, lining up behind their leader.

5 When all the players have chosen a team, they'll end up in two long lines facing each other, with the leaders at the front.

6 They hold each other by the waist and have a tug-of-war between the two teams. Usually everyone ends up on the ground!

The words of the Bulgarian song translate as, "Open the doors, Your Majesty. From here the Royal Army will pass. Open, close, take one of us." Why not make up your own song for this game?

PEHME KAPSAS

Perhaps you've lived your entire life without ever feeling the need to act like a cabbage? Well, this Estonian game will give you the chance! Its name means "soft cabbage."

ESTONIA | INDOORS OR OUTDOORS | NO EQUIPMENT | GUESSING GAME | 6+ PLAYERS

Thief

Cabbages grow well in Estonia's climate. They are used in soups, stews, salads, and dumplings, and their leaves are also used to wrap spicy minced meat.

1 Choose one player to be the gardener and one to be the thief. The rest will be cabbages.

2 The gardener secretly tells each cabbage what kind of cabbage they will be: strong or soft. They all sit in the "garden."

Gardener

3 The thief arrives and has to make up a funny reason for needing to go into the garden. Once inside, they test all the cabbages by pressing down on their heads. If they are soft, they will slump. The thief takes the strong cabbages back to their base.

4 The gardener tells the remaining cabbages whether they will be soft or strong, and the thief comes back.

5 The game continues until the thief has taken all the cabbages!

The best thing about this game is the silly stories that the thief must invent in order to convince the gardener to let them in and to distract the gardener while they test the cabbages. Use your acting skills and let your imagination run wild!

THE HANDKERCHIEF

When you have an odd number of players, you can't divide into equal teams. This game from Greece is a perfect solution for that situation—and the "extra" player has a very important role to play!

GREECE | **OUTDOORS** | **HANDKERCHIEFS** | **ACTIVE PLAY** | **9+ PLAYERS**

1 Divide the group into two equal teams. One person will be the leader instead of being on a team.

2 Each team lines up at opposite ends of the space, with the leader in the middle.

3 On each team, everyone is secretly assigned a number, starting with one. There will be a player on the other team who has the same number.

4 The leader holds up a handkerchief and calls out a number. The player on each team with that number runs and tries to get the handkerchief.

5 If a player grabs the handkerchief and makes it back to their team's line without getting tagged, they get to keep the handkerchief. If the other player tags them before they reach safety, then they get to keep it instead.

6 The game ends when all the handkerchiefs have been won. The team with the most is the winner!

Games and sport in Greece have a very long history. In fact, the modern Olympic Games are based on sporting contests that were held in Greece almost 3,000 years ago!

MAKE YOUR OWN!

You're now an expert on games from around the world! The games in this book should keep you and your friends busy for weeks, but if you ever run out of things to do, why not try to make up your own game? Work together with your friends to invent something that everyone can enjoy playing.

TYPES OF GAMES

What kind of game do you like best?
There are many different types in this book.

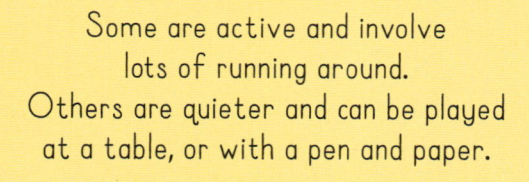

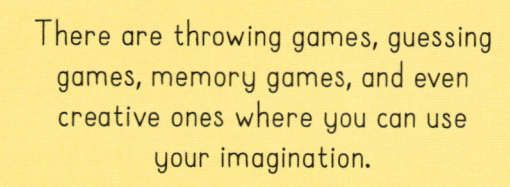

Some are active and involve lots of running around. Others are quieter and can be played at a table, or with a pen and paper.

There are throwing games, guessing games, memory games, and even creative ones where you can use your imagination.

HOW MANY?

How many players do you have? Some games work better with lots of people, while others need just a few. If you're making a game for a big group, make sure that everyone has an interesting role to play, so no one gets bored. Try to arrange it so that all the players get a turn to be leader or "it."

KEEP IT SIMPLE

Have you ever tried out a new board game, but had to spend so long reading the rules that you were bored before you even started to play? Don't fall into this trap and make your game too complicated! The best games are simple enough that you can learn the rules in just a few minutes. That makes it quick to teach new players who want to join in.

OVER TO YOU!

Are you ready to make up your own game? You may need to try a few ideas before you find one that really works. Your friends can help you think up ideas and fix any problems. And don't forget that although many games have a winner and a loser, the main goal is to have fun!

63

INDEX

active play 11, 15, 29-30, 32, 34-39, 41, 43-44, 46-48, 50-57, 59, 61
Australia 18
Austria 47

ball games 18, 35, 39, 54
big groups, games for 42-61
blind man's buff 50-51
board games 12, 25
Brazil 15, 22
Bulgaria 59

Canada 20
catch the dragon's tail 52
ceviz oyunu 31
Chile 47, 56
China 8, 13, 52
choose the stone 17
Colombia 55
conkers 21
corre, corre la guaraca 56
creative play 19

dance 30
ddakji 26
dithwai 33
down, down, down 18
duck, duck, goose 57

equipment 7
Estonia 60
exquisite corpse 19

feuer, wasser, sturm, blitz 36
fighting serpents 25
France 9, 19, 47, 54, 57

Germany 36, 47, 49
Ghana 43
ghost in the graveyard 41
Greece 61
guessing game 40

hajla 32
halászás 53

handkerchief, the 61
hide-and-seek 29, 38, 41
hopscotch 32
Hungary 52

imbube imbube 50
India 48
Indonesia 12
Israel 47
"it" 8, 29, 34-35, 50-51, 56-57, 63
Italy 29

Japan 9, 27
jegichagi 11
jogo da cabra-cega 51
jogo dos pés atados 37
juguemos en el bosque 55

kabaddi 48
kolowis awithlaknannai 25

la tomate 54
le facteur n'est pas passé 57
Lesotho 33
Liberia 17
luta de galo 22

make the stick jump 20
making up your own game 62-63
Marco Polo 51
memory game 33
Mexico 14
muurball 39

nascondino 29
Netherlands 9, 39, 47
New Zealand 47

one-player games 10-15
oonch neech 44
open the doors, your majesty 59

Pakistan 44
party games 45, 49, 58
pass the parcel 45

pehme kapsas 60
Philippines 30
pilolo 43
play fighting 21, 22
Poland 23, 40
Portugal 37, 51
posición en latas 15
puzzle games 13, 14, 17

Rochambeau 9
rock-paper-scissors 8-9

salonowiec 40
sardines 38
schokoladenessen 49
serso 23
shiritori 27
Singapore 47
South Korea 11, 26, 47
statues 46-47
stilts 15
Sweden 24
Syria 32

tag 34-35, 46-47, 48, 50-51
tangrams 13
tchuka ruma 12
telephone 58
three- to five-player games 28-41
throwing games 18, 20, 23, 24, 26, 31
tied feet race 37
tinikling 30
tripas de gato 14
Turkey 31
two-player games 16-27

United Kingdom 21, 38, 45, 47
United States 20, 25, 41, 47, 51, 57

Viking Chess 24

where to play 6
word game 27

64